Let this Book empowere you as a women. Let it release the very power of a vertuouse women that God invested in you.

Love Junine

xxx

PRESENTED TO:

A wonderfull women called
Linda

We love Him because He first loved us.

1 JOHN 4:19 NKJV

PRESENTED BY:

From the daughter of your
soul Lunine

DATE:

14th of May 2007

ADORED
BY GOD

Harrison House
Tulsa, Oklahoma

Declarations for Your Life written by James Riddle.

Compilation, writing, and composition of devotions by Christy Phillippe in association with Bordon Books, Tulsa, Oklahoma.

10 09 08 07 06   10 9 8 7 6 5 4 3 2 1

Adored by God
ISBN 1-57794-802-5
Copyright © 2006 by Harrison House, Inc.

Published by **Harrison House, Inc.**
P.O. Box 35035
Tulsa, Oklahoma 74153

INTRODUCTION

God not only loves you, but absolutely adores you! He was intimately involved in your creation. Psalm 139:13 says that He knit you together in your mother's womb.

But He didn't stop there. He watched over your life and protected you until the day you became part of His family. And now He delights in you and longs to give you the desires of your heart.

Draw near to Him as you read the pages of this book. Allow Him to wrap His loving arms around you. He stands ready to shower you with His blessings, His love, and His grace. You are truly *adored by God*.

You Are a Miracle!

 very newborn baby is a miracle—tiny fingers and fingernails, adorable toes, perfectly shaped nose and mouth. God is the One who creates such a miracle. Every child, and adult, is just as amazing to Him, no matter their age or circumstances in life.

God's love covered you when you were still in your mother's womb, and His love still covers you today. He was intimately and intricately involved in your creation, and just as He formed your physical body, He wants to be involved in the rest of your life, as well. God has great plans for you, and He longs to help you fulfill the destiny for which He created you! Invite Him right now into all those important details of your life.

I praise you because I am fearfully and
  wonderfully made;
your works are wonderful,
I know that full well.

PSALM 139:14

DECLARATION FOR YOUR LIFE

I am fearfully and wonderfully made, and God is very proud to call me His child. I know that I am a very special and unique individual with a grand purpose and destiny in this life.

A Glorious Future

hatever plans you have made for your life, God's plans for you are even better. He has chosen you and has only good things in store for you. You can rest assured and be confident that He is not out to harm you. No, His plans for you are good—entirely good—in every way!

Take the time to thank Him today for His goodness to you. Ask Him to reveal His good plans for your life. Look forward to your future with great hope, because God's great love for you and His supernatural power are at work in your life. He will bring His good plans for you to pass.

"For I know the plans I have for you,"
declares the Lord, "plans to prosper
you and not to harm you, plans to
give you hope and a future."

JEREMIAH 29:11

DECLARATION FOR YOUR LIFE

*All of God's thoughts for me are for good and never
evil. His plan for my life is to make me prosperous, give
me hope, and provide for me a glorious future. He has
handpicked everything that is best for me in life and
presents it to me with great joy. His desire for me is to
live in His abundance.*

ong before you were ever conceived in your mother's womb, long before you took your first breath, spoke your first word, took your first step, God knew you and loved you so much that He set in motion a plan that would allow you to be with Him forever.

Long before you ever sinned, God set the rescue plan in motion—Jesus came to this earth and died so that you could live with God forever. You are cherished, deeply loved by the Creator of the universe, and He wants you to spend all of eternity with Him. All He asks is that you believe in Him and entrust the reins of your heart and life into His loving hands.

For God so loved the world, that he gave
his only begotten Son, that whosoever
believeth in him should not perish,
but have everlasting life.

JOHN 3:16 KJV

DECLARATION FOR YOUR LIFE

God looked down across the ages, saw me, took pity on my spiritually dead condition, and so dearly loved me that He gave His only begotten Son, Jesus, so that I would not perish, but have everlasting life.

ver 100 years ago, a tornado struck the prairies of Minnesota. Many were killed, hundreds were injured, and one small town was almost demolished. In the midst of the disaster, an elderly British surgeon and his two medically trained sons worked around the clock for days aiding the stricken, bandaging wounds, and setting broken limbs.

Their heroic work did not go unnoticed. The doctor and his sons were offered financial backing to build a hospital. The men agreed and in 1889 founded a clinic. The elderly doctor's name: William W. Mayo.

From a great tragedy, the Mayo Clinic was born. It now consists of over 500 physicians treating more than 200,000 people a year and is known worldwide as one of the premiere clinics of health and excellence in medicine. God is not the author of disaster, but He is able to supernaturally turn negative situations around for good. What situation can you invite God into today?

We know that in all things God works for the good of those who love him, who have been called according to his purpose.

ROMANS 8:28

DECLARATION FOR YOUR LIFE

With God Himself as my prayer partner, I know that everything I am praying for in the Spirit [under the Holy Spirit's direction] will work together for my good. My Father has given me a specific purpose in His great plan and I joyfully fulfill it in my life.

THE DIVINE ERASER

 little girl who was watching a plane skywrite letters in the clouds was puzzled when the letters faded and slowly disappeared. Then suddenly the answer came to her: "Maybe Jesus has an eraser!"

Her innocent wisdom conveys an important truth. Just as skywriting disappears into the sky, so Jesus can wipe away the sins that we so bitterly regret. With God's forgiveness they will fade away. What sins do you need to confess this day? Rest assured: Jesus *does* have an eraser.

If we confess our sins, he is faithful and just and will forgive us our sins and purify us from all unrighteousness.

1 JOHN 1:9

DECLARATION FOR YOUR LIFE

I freely admit that I have sinned. Therefore, being faithful and just, God has forgiven all of my sin and cleansed me from all unrighteousness. In this, I bring honor to God, and His Word has a secure place in my life.

n England, a charming old cottage held a little wall plaque that read "Why Pray When You Can Worry?" There is some humor in that statement, but it would be better to live out the phrase "Why Worry When You Can Pray?"

The second question holds important truths. When the Scriptures tell you to pray without ceasing, it is literally an invitation to cooperate with God in the details of your life.

Instead of worrying about your problems, ask God to intervene and lift the burden from your shoulders. Instead of only thinking creatively about how to get yourself out of a situation, pray creatively about what God's solution might be. When you release your worries to God, He takes over and can work all things out to your benefit.

Seek first his kingdom and his righteousness, and all these things will be given to you as well…. Do not worry about tomorrow, for tomorrow will worry about itself.

MATTHEW 6:33-34

DECLARATION FOR YOUR LIFE

I absolutely refuse to worry! I will have plenty to eat, plenty to drink, and plenty to wear. I do not crave these things selfishly and focus my attention on obtaining them, while neglecting God's kingdom. I simply rejoice in the present fact of my Father's provision.

One of the deadliest earthquakes to strike Iran filled that nation with sadness. But in the midst of despair, one story gave people hope. Cradled in her dead mother's arms, surrounded by the crumbled remnant of a collapsed building, a baby girl was found alive. The mother had shielded six-month-old Nassim from the falling debris and saved her life. Rescuers found the girl thirty-seven hours after the earthquake. Said the Red Cross public-relations deputy director in Tehran: "She is alive because of her mother's embrace."

Those who take refuge in Jesus' embrace are shielded from sin's devastating impact, saved through His sacrifice, and protected by His love. If you allow Him to, God's love will shelter your life.

He who dwells in the shelter of the
Most High
will rest in the shadow of the Almighty.
I will say of the Lord, "He is my refuge
and my fortress,
my God, in whom I trust."

PSALM 91:1–2

DECLARATION FOR YOUR LIFE

I dwell in the secret place of the Most High and rest,
remaining steadfast and secure, under the shadow of
the Almighty. He is my refuge and my fortress, my God
and Father, and I trust Him with all of my heart.

EVEN IN THE DETAILS

ne night Susan went into her eight-year-old daughter's bedroom to pray with her before she went to sleep. In the course of her prayer, she said, "Jesus, please lock the doors if they haven't been locked." Susan held back a chuckle at her unexpected request and thought nothing more about it. The next morning, however, she opened the front door to find the keys outside in the lock. She stood amazed at how the Lord had led her little girl to pray—and thanked Him for His protection.

Even in the little details, God is concerned about your life—why not entrust them to Him today?

You will not fear the terror of night,
  nor the arrow that flies by day,
nor the pestilence that stalks in the darkness,
  nor the plague that destroys at midday.

PSALM 91:5–6

DECLARATION FOR YOUR LIFE

I do not fear the terror of the night, nor the arrow that flies by day, nor the pestilence that stalks in the darkness, nor the plague that lays waste at noonday. A thousand may fall at my side, even ten thousand at my right hand, but it shall not come near me.

ngels are all around us, God's heavenly warriors, dispatched on our behalf. As Billy Graham has stated: "Christians should never fail to sense the operation of angelic glory. It forever eclipses the world of demonic powers, as the sun does a candle's light."

In what ways do you or your loved ones need angelic help or protection? God is faithful to save us as we speak forth His Word and trust our lives into His loving care. Place God's heavenly angels around you this day to guard and protect you in all your ways.

He shall give his angels charge over thee,
to keep thee in all thy ways. They shall
bear thee up in their hands, lest thou
dash thy foot against a stone.

PSALM 91:11–12 KJV

DECLARATION FOR YOUR LIFE

God has commanded the angels to set up camp around me as sentinels in my life. They guard me in all of my ways and keep me from all harm. They bear me up in their hands lest I dash my foot against a stone.

ate one night, a man in Slim Cornett's church was showing Slim around a county airport in rural Mississippi. "This switch lights up the runway," the man said as he flipped it. "Then, let's say there is a plane in distress up there. I would throw this switch and turn on the searchlights."

As the night skies lit up, a small plane material- ized out of the darkness and landed. Slim and his friend watched in amazement as Franklin Graham, son of the famous evangelist, stepped off the plane. The pilot had been flying Franklin back to school in Texas when the electrical system shut down, leaving them stranded in the Mississippi night without lights or radio or any means of guidance. From out of nowhere, the search beam had come on and guided them to the landing strip.

Earlier that evening before they left home, Billy Graham had prayed for the Father to protect and guide his son and the pilot. God answered his prayer in a miraculous way—and He offers you the same protection and guidance this day.

"Because he loves me," says the Lord, "I will
rescue him;
I will protect him, for he acknowledges
my name.
He will call upon me, and I will answer him;
I will be with him in trouble,
I will deliver him and honor him.
With long life will I satisfy him
and show him my salvation."

PSALM 91:14–16

DECLARATION FOR YOUR LIFE

*God has made a decree (a fixed law) concerning me, saying,
"I will rescue him/her from every calamity; I will protect
him/her because he/she acknowledges My name. He/She
will call upon Me and I will answer him/her. I will be with
him/her in times of trouble. I will deliver him/her and set
him/her in the place of highest honor. With long life will I
satisfy him/her and show him/her My salvation."*

GOOD THINGS ON THE WAY

our-year-old Josh was visiting his grandparents. His grandmother told him he could have cereal, pancakes, or waffles for breakfast.

He thought a minute, looked up at his grandmother, and then asked, "Did you say cookies?"

The philosopher Epictetus once said: "Contentment comes not so much from great wealth as from few wants." God was wise to tell us to delight ourselves in Him first—and allow Him to refine the desires of our hearts. He longs to give us only good things—but we must trust Him to know exactly what those good things are.

What are the desires of your heart? God wants only good things for you—and He is trustworthy to fulfill His good plans for your life.

Delight yourself in the Lord
   and he will give you the desires of
     your heart.
Commit your way to the Lord;
   trust in him and he will do this:
He will make your righteousness shine like
    the dawn,
   the justice of your cause like the
    noonday sun.

PSALM 37:4–6

DECLARATION FOR YOUR LIFE

I stand for what is good and right and trust in the Lord with unfailing loyalty. He is my comfort and my delight, and He gives me all the desires of my heart. My way is committed to Him, to trust in Him in every circumstance. He will make my righteousness shine like the dawn, and the justice of my cause will blaze like the noonday sun.

nurse neglected to tell her new patient, a little boy, how his hospital intercom worked. Soon his light flashed. When the nurse called the boy's name and asked what he wanted, there was complete silence. The nurse repeated herself. After a long pause, the little boy said, "Jesus, I hear You, but I don't see You. Where are You?"

If we have trusted Jesus to be our Lord and Savior, the Holy Spirit's presence is always with us and our steps will be ordered by Him. Everywhere you go this day and in everything you do, be aware that God is with you.

If the Lord delights in a man's way,
   he makes his steps firm;
though he stumble, he will not fall,
   for the Lord upholds him with his hand.

PSALM 37:23–24

DECLARATION FOR YOUR LIFE

*My Father is overjoyed to spend His time with me. He
rejoices as we walk this life together, and He sees to it
that all of my steps stand firm. Even if I stumble, I will
not fall, for the Lord will catch me with His hand.*

here is a marvelous little book written by a former shepherd that tells about his experience as a shepherd in East Africa. The land adjacent to his was rented out to a tenant who didn't take very good care of his sheep: His land was overgrazed, eaten down to the ground; the sheep were thin, diseased by parasites, and attacked by wild animals. The author especially remembered how the neighbor's sheep would line up at the fence and blankly stare in the direction of his green grass and his healthy sheep, almost as if they yearned to be delivered from their abusive shepherd. They longed to come to the other side of the fence and belong to him.

The identity of the Shepherd is everything. It is wonderful to be able to say, "The Lord is my Shepherd"!

The Lord is my shepherd, I shall not be
in want.
He makes me lie down in green pastures,
he leads me beside quiet waters.

PSALM 23:1–2

DECLARATION FOR YOUR LIFE

*The Lord is my Shepherd, a fierce guardian who
watches over me with a relentless eye. He fills all of my
needs and desires so that I am in want of nothing. He
makes me to lie down in green pastures—a fertile land
of abundance. He leads me beside the still and quiet
streams of life-giving water.*

od is more willing to bestow His blessings on us than we are to receive them!

Heavenly Father,

You are my Shepherd, the all-sufficient One who meets every need that I could ever have. Teach me to rely on You and Your Word for all that I need in this life. Your green pastures and still waters are more satisfying than anything this world could ever offer. Help me to follow You closely and walk in Your ways. In Jesus' name. Amen.

He restores my soul.
He guides me in paths of righteousness
for his name's sake.

Psalm 23:3

Declaration for Your Life

The Lord restores my life to full vitality. He guides me
in the paths of righteousness for His name's sake alone
and not by my own merits.

istening to a student read the Scripture in seminary chapel, Joseph Sittler, now blind, heard something he'd never heard before: "Yea, though I walk through the valley of the shadow of death, I will fear no evil, for Thou art with me."

"The text does not speak," said Sittler, "of the valley of death but the valley of the shadow of death. There is a difference. The wonderful truth is that God is with us now. It is not simply that God will be with us in the experience of death itself; it is that God will walk with us through all of *life.*"

As you walk out God's plan for your life, realize that He is with you, in both the shadows and the light. He cares about everything that concerns you.

Even though I walk
   through the valley of the shadow of death,
I will fear no evil,
   for you are with me;
your rod and your staff,
   they comfort me.

PSALM 23:4

DECLARATION FOR YOUR LIFE

Even if I am walking in the midst of death's domain,
I will fear no evil, for I know that the Lord is with me.

n elderly but still dynamic Billy Graham spoke at a luncheon in January 2002 and said these words: "See the suit I'm wearing? It's a brand-new suit. My wife, children, and my grandchildren are telling me I've gotten a little slovenly. I used to be a bit more fastidious. So I went out and bought a new suit for this luncheon and one more occasion. Do you know what that occasion is? This is the suit in which I'll be buried. But when you hear I'm dead, I don't want you to immediately remember the suit I'm wearing. I want you to remember this: I not only know who I am—but I also know where I'm going."

Thank God today for the assurance of your salvation—that you know that you know you'll go to heaven when you die to spend all of eternity in His presence.

Surely goodness and love will follow me
   all the days of my life,
and I will dwell in the house of the Lord
   forever.

PSALM 23:6

DECLARATION FOR YOUR LIFE

The Lord's love and His mercy cling to me all the days
of my life, and He calls me His own forevermore.

GOD'S HANDS ARE BIGGER

 young boy went to the local candy store with his mother. The shop owner, a kindly old man, passed him a large jar of lollipops and invited him to help himself to a handful. When the boy said no, the shopkeeper reached in and pulled out a handful for the boy.

When outside, the boy's mother asked why he had suddenly been so shy and wouldn't reach into the jar when the man had offered.

The boy replied, "Because his hands are so much bigger than mine!" The man was able to hold a greater amount of candy than the boy ever could.

God's hands are so much bigger than ours! Allow Him to bless you in the ways He sees fit and you'll be surprised at how "pleasant" your inheritance will be.

Lord, you have assigned me my portion and
my cup;
you have made my lot secure.
The boundary lines have fallen for me in
pleasant places;
surely I have a delightful inheritance.

PSALM 16:5–6

DECLARATION FOR YOUR LIFE

My heavenly Father has assigned me my share of His inheritance and my cup overflows continually. He has set my boundaries in a spacious and pleasant land and has given me a delightful endowment.

hen Jerome Groopman diagnosed patients with serious diseases, the Harvard medical school professor discovered that all of them were "looking for a sense of genuine hope, and indeed, that hope was as important to them as anything he might prescribe as a physician."

When asked for his definition of *hope*, he replied: "Basically, I think hope is the ability to see a path to the future. You are facing dire circumstances, and you need to know everything that's blocking or threatening you. And then you see a path, or a potential path, to get where you want to be."

The doctor confessed: "I think hope has been, is, and always will be the heart of medicine and healing. We could not live without hope." In what do you place your hope today? When you hope in God's mercy, you will never be disappointed.

The Lord takes pleasure in those who
    fear Him,
In those who hope in His mercy.

PSALM 147:11 NKJV

DECLARATION FOR YOUR LIFE

I bring my Father great joy just because I'm me. I rest in His mercy and have hope.

o many people it is more important to be loved than to love. When we do not have the experience of being loved by God, just as we are and not as we should be, then loving others can become a duty, a responsibility, a chore. But if we allow ourselves to be loved just as we are, with the love of God poured into our hearts by the Holy Spirit, then we can reach out to others in a more effortless way.

We love—because He first loved us!

We love because he first loved us.

1 JOHN 4:19

DECLARATION FOR YOUR LIFE

God is love. As I live in God, I live in love, and God lives in me.

The Pilot

 eff was invited by a friend to fly across central Florida in his private plane. During his friend's 50 years of experience as a pilot, he had flown all over the world and faced every possible condition.

On their return trip, the airplane began to shake and the engine started losing power. Terror gripped Jeff. There was nothing he could do. He had no experience in flying, landing—or fixing—a plane.

Then Jeff looked at his friend who sat at the controls. He was utterly calm as he adjusted knobs and continued to pilot the plane to a safe landing.

There are times in life when we desperately want to grab control. Jeff's experience in the plane reminded him that if he insists on control he could ruin or destroy his life. At those moments, we must resist the urge to control and trust the One who has seen it all before, and who knows what He is doing.

[Jesus said], Let not your heart be troubled:
ye believe in God, believe also in me.

JOHN 14:1 KJV

DECLARATION FOR YOUR LIFE

I will not allow my heart to become troubled, distressed, or terrified. I believe in my Father and I believe in Jesus.

xplorer Ernest Shackleton headed an expedition to the South Pole. Near the end of their journey, food supplies were exhausted save for one last ration of hardtack that was distributed to each man, some of whom saved it for later. After the weary men had gone to sleep, Shackleton said that out of the corner of his eye, he noticed one of his most trusted men looking about to see if anyone was watching.

Shackleton's heart sank within him as this man began to reach toward the sack of the man next to him. The man then opened the sack, took his own hardtack, and put it into the other man's sack.

The Lord wants to satisfy the deepest hungers that you have—body, soul, and spirit. He has taken His own "bread" and placed it into your "sack." Trust in Him and you will never hunger or thirst again.

Jesus said to them, "I am the bread of life.
He who comes to Me shall never hunger,
and he who believes in Me shall never thirst."

JOHN 6:35 NKJV

DECLARATION FOR YOUR LIFE

Jesus is the Bread of Life to me. I cling to Him with all of my heart. Because of Him, I will never hunger or thirst again.

n 1986, two brothers who lived in a kibbutz near the Sea of Galilee made an incredible discovery. As these two Israeli fishermen monitored their equipment on the beaches of Gennesaret, they noticed something they'd not seen before. Something covered with mud glistened in the sun. Upon examination, archaeologists determined that what the brothers had discovered was a fishing boat dating from the time of Jesus—an incredibly valuable find. The only reason the artifact was discovered was because of a three-year drought, resulting in unusually low water in the lake.

God's love for you is so strong that even when you least expect it, God can uncover things of amazing value in your life.

We can be so sure that every detail in
our lives of love for God is worked
into something good.

ROMANS 8:28 THE MESSAGE

DECLARATION FOR YOUR LIFE

*God cares about the details of my life. He will take
any bad experience I may have and turn it around
for good.*

PLEASING HIM

 certain drug addict turned his life around when he accepted Jesus. Several weeks after making a commitment to God, the craving for drugs became overwhelming and he hit the streets searching for his former dealers. In his desperation he cried out to the Lord to help him. All of a sudden it was as if his feet were moving all by themselves. He found himself back at his home and the insatiable desire had left.

When you call out to God, He will work through you in amazing ways. He will help you to do what is right—to do His good pleasure.

Jesus said,… "The one who sent me is
with me; he has not left me alone,
for I always do what pleases him."

JOHN 8:28–29

DECLARATION FOR YOUR LIFE

*I continually walk in the ways of my heavenly Father,
and He looks upon me with tremendous joy and
delight. In everything that I do and say, I give Him
glory. He is ever with me, working both in and
through me, to will and do His good pleasure.*

uring the recent uprisings in the Middle East, Ron and Jake Jones, who serve with the Christian and Missionary Alliance in Israel, communicated the following in their prayer letter:

> *Yesterday a friend shared with us something she observed that was a delightful reminder of God's care for us. She watched a shepherd caring for his flock near the area where guns are fired. Every time the shots rang out the sheep scattered in fright. The shepherd then touched each of them with his staff and spoke calmly. The sheep settled down immediately because they trusted the shepherd. Each time the guns sounded, the sheep needed the shepherd to orient them again and reassure them they were safe.*

Just like these sheep, our Shepherd longs to reach out and touch us with His love, to speak words of calm and comfort in difficult times.

Jesus said,… "I am the gate for the sheep. All who ever came before me were thieves and robbers, but the sheep did not listen to them. I am the gate; whoever enters through me will be saved. He will come in and go out, and find pasture."

JOHN 10:7–9

DECLARATION FOR YOUR LIFE

Jesus is the Door for the sheep. I enter God's blessings and salvation through Him alone. I am one of the true sheep. Jesus is the Door and I have entered through Him into this mighty covenant communion with God that I now enjoy. In Him, I enjoy true freedom and liberty, and I find such pasture that whatever the circumstance, good or bad, I have all that I need and more.

THE GOOD SHEPHERD

s a young mother, one Christmas brought Brenda to despair. Amid the holiday stress, her husband's job was shaky and times were tough. She writes:

Among my numerous responsibilities was teaching my three-year-old's Sunday-school class at church. When I looked at the teacher's book, I saw that the lesson was on Jesus, the Good Shepherd. What? The Good Shepherd? I complained. Surely something is wrong here. City kids can't relate to a shepherd!

The time came for class. We survived the art portion of the lesson, gluing cotton balls to sheep pictures, and had our juice and animal crackers. Then it was circle time. Turning to each rosy-cheeked cherub, I began with, "What is a good shepherd?" To which came my reminder of truth as one tot positively replied, "He picks up his sheep when they fall down."

God's plans for you include an amazing, abundant life. And as the Good Shepherd, He carefully watches over you to bring those good plans to pass.

[Jesus said], "The thief comes only to steal and kill and destroy; I have come that they may have life, and have it to the full. I am the good shepherd. The good shepherd lays down his life for the sheep."

JOHN 10:10–11

DECLARATION FOR YOUR LIFE

I know that the thief comes only to steal, kill, and destroy. Jesus, on the other hand, came to give me the life of God with all of its abundance (provision overflowing and bursting through the seams). Jesus is such a Good Shepherd to me. He so loves me that He willingly laid down His life to provide for me all that He has and all that He is.

"Good Morning" in Heaven

id you know that Winston Churchill planned his own funeral? At the service in St. Paul's Cathedral, there were stately hymns and an impressive liturgy. But at the end of the service, Churchill had an unusual event planned. After they said the benediction, a bugler high in the dome of the cathedral played "Taps," the universal signal that the day is over. There was a long pause. Then a bugler on the other side played "Reveille," the military wake-up call.

It was Churchill's way of communicating that, while we say "Good night" here, it's "Good morning" in heaven. Now, why would he do that? Because he believed in Jesus Christ, who said, "I am the resurrection and the life."

Jesus said,… "I am the resurrection and the life. He who believes in Me, though he may die, he shall live. And whoever lives and believes in Me shall never die."

JOHN 11:25–26 NKJV

DECLARATION FOR YOUR LIFE

Jesus is my resurrection and my life. All that I am, in spirit, is found in Him. And although I may die in the flesh [after living out the fullness of my days in this earth], I will live on in the spirit for all of eternity.

ark was one of those kids who needed to hear the Gospel—and it happened at church camp, but not in the expected way.

Bob Mitchell, the main speaker that week, called most of the shots—including when meals would be served. So "Mitch" was always talking with the cook.

The cook loved her work, but it was exhausting. She always looked tired. Whenever she talked to Mitch, he got up and gave her his chair—and a moment's rest—while they discussed meal plans. Nobody noticed Mitch doing this—except Mark. Later that week, Mark asked Jesus to be his Savior. It wasn't because of the messages, Mark said, but because of the love he saw exemplified in Mitch's life.

God's love is simple—unconditional, "no-matter-what" love that He wants us to receive from Him and then show to each other. You never know who might be watching.

Dear friends, let us love one another, for love comes from God. Everyone who loves has been born of God and knows God.

1 JOHN 4:7

DECLARATION FOR YOUR LIFE

I show my love for the body of Christ continually. All of my ability to love comes from God. As I am in Him, and He in me, His love pours forth from me in abundance. I love because I have been born of God and know Him.

wo brothers shared a mill, each night dividing the grain they had ground together during the day. One brother lived alone; the other had a large family.

The single brother thought, *It isn't fair that we divide the grain evenly. My brother has children to feed.* So each night he secretly put some of his grain into his brother's granary.

The married brother said to himself, *It isn't fair that we divide the grain evenly. I have children who will care for me in my old age; my brother has none.* So each night he secretly gave some of his grain to his brother, as well.

One night they met halfway between their houses. They realized what was happening and embraced each other in love.

God has met you halfway—and He longs to pour out His love upon you. Won't you open your heart to receive His blessings today?

This is how God showed his love among us:
He sent his one and only Son into
the world that we might live through him.
This is love: not that we loved God,
but that he loved us and sent his Son
as an atoning sacrifice for our sins.

1 JOHN 4:9–10

DECLARATION FOR YOUR LIFE

God showed His own love for me by sending Jesus into the world so that I might live through Him. This is love in its purest form—not that I instigated this love relationship I now enjoy with the Father, but He loved me so much that He sent Jesus to me. He did this so that He could turn His wrath away from me and make me His own son/daughter. Indeed, I am forgiven of all sin and am now the very son/daughter of almighty God!

GOD IS "FOR" YOU!

od is love. Jesus loves me. These are simple truths that most of us know in our heads—but not in our hearts. God loves you more than your human mind could ever imagine.

In the gospel we discover that we are far worse off than we thought—but we are far more loved than we ever dreamed. Jesus paid the highest price so that we can live with Him forever. The Good News of the gospel is that God is "for" us—and He will do whatever it takes to show us His love!

Dear heavenly Father,

Thank You so much for Your love for me. No matter what I have done or how I have failed You, You still care for me. I confess that Jesus is the Son of God and that He died to save me from my sins. Thank You for everything You have done for me. Amen.

Whosoever shall confess that Jesus is
the Son of God, God dwelleth in him,
and he in God. And we have known
and believed the love that God hath to us.
God is love; and he that dwelleth in love
dwelleth in God, and God in him.

1 JOHN 4:15–16 KJV

DECLARATION FOR YOUR LIFE

*I acknowledge that Jesus is the Son of God; therefore,
God lives in me and I in Him. I both know and rely
upon the love that God has for me. God is love. As I
live in God, I live in love, and God lives in me.*

The children's television-show host Mister Rogers once said, "Love is deep and simple, but what our society gives is shallow and complicated." God's love is perhaps the simplest of all—unconditional, "no-matter-what" love that God wants us to receive from Him and then show to each other.

This kind of love cannot peacefully "coexist" with fear. When you discover—and really, truly understand—the kind of love that God has for you, there is no reason left to fear. He has wonderful, amazing plans for your life; He will protect you from all evil; He guards your life and will bring His purposes for you to pass. These are powerful truths that you can stand on. And when you do, fear disappears!

There is no fear in love; but perfect love casteth out fear: because fear hath torment. He that feareth is not made perfect in love.

1 John 4:18 KJV

Declaration for Your Life

I will allow no fear, terror, worry, or anxiety to enter my life for any reason whatsoever, for there is no fear in love. God is on my side in any and every circumstance. He is always for me, and never against me.

hen Pat Reilly visited a new church for the first time, he had an experience that taught him a lesson about prayer. After the service Reilly lingered, talking to this person and that. When he stepped outside, his four-year-old daughter, Melody, was still inside the building. By then the building was empty, and the door was locked and could only be opened with a key.

Pat called through the mail slot in the large oak door, "Melody, are you in there?" A small frightened voice answered, "Yes, Daddy." Then Melody put her hand through the mail slot so her father could hold it until someone fetched a key. Melody could not see him, but she knew her father was there, and she was comforted.

Prayer is like a comforting hand through a mail slot. The Father is there listening even when you can't see Him. When you call upon Him and seek His face, He is sure to answer!

Then shall ye call upon me, and ye
shall go and pray unto me, and I will
hearken unto you. And ye shall seek me,
and find me, when ye shall search
for me with all your heart.

JEREMIAH 29:12–13 KJV

DECLARATION FOR YOUR LIFE

*My call brings a smile to my Father's face and He
listens to me with great concern. When I seek Him with
all of my heart, He sees to it that I find Him. He has
rescued me from the powers of darkness and is now
enjoying my continual companionship.*

od loves you with an everlasting love—
it will never end, no matter what
condition you are in.

David Slagle's 21-month-old, who had just learned
to say "Daddy," had been struggling with asthma and
an ear infection for two weeks. He coughed and
sneezed continually, and his nose ran like a faucet. Each
night when David came home, his son ran to meet him
at the door, smiling, coughing, nose running, and
calling, "Daddy! Daddy!" David was not repulsed by his
runny nose or close-range sneezes in the least. He
loved his son and enjoyed his son's love for him.

God is the same way. No matter what is happening in your life, you can always run to Him as a child
to its father, calling, "Father, Father!"

The Lord appeared from of old to me … ,
saying, Yes, I have loved you with an
everlasting love; therefore with loving-
kindness have I drawn you and
continued My faithfulness to you.

JEREMIAH 31:3 AMP

DECLARATION FOR YOUR LIFE

*My heavenly Father loves me with an eternal devotion
and has drawn me to Himself with immeasurable
compassion. I have His word that He will mold me
and make me what He desires me to be. From here on
out, He will do nothing but encourage, strengthen, and
build me up. I can rest assured that He will never give
up on me.*

A Prayer of Gratitude

ord, I don't know where I'd be without Your loving hand guiding me. I need You so much! Thank You for blotting out my transgressions! I am so thankful for Your presence in my life, and Your great faithfulness to me. Your loving-kindness has changed my life. You are the stability and the security of my life. You are the greatest treasure of my heart. So, I will trust You in the days ahead. I now receive Your strength, and I thank You for Your watchful care and protection over my life. I rejoice that I belong to You forever. Amen.

[The Lord says],

"I, even I, am he who blots out

your transgressions, for my own sake,

and remembers your sins no more."

ISAIAH 43:25

DECLARATION FOR YOUR LIFE

God has blotted out my transgressions for only one reason: He loves me. Never again will He remember the foolishness of my past.

od's love for you is eternal—it will never end. Even when you leave this earth, He will take you to a place that He is already preparing for you.

What makes heaven, heaven is not streets made of gold or beautiful mansions. Heaven is far greater than our wildest imagination. The same God who designed the best of everything in this world also designed heaven, only He took it to a far greater extent than anything we've ever seen. Yet that's not even what makes heaven, heaven—instead, it's God, being there with Him. With His presence comes peace and contentment, fulfillment, and joy. We can anticipate this future in the presence of God, but we can also experience God's presence now, here on earth. When you spend time with your heavenly Father, He will fill you with joy and wonderful peace. God's love will shower your life with blessings in this life and in the life to come!

Place me like a seal over your heart,
   like a seal on your arm;
for love is as strong as death....
Many waters cannot quench love;
   rivers cannot wash it away.

SONG OF SONGS 8:6–7

DECLARATION FOR YOUR LIFE

*I am placed like a seal over the Lord's heart—like a
signet on His arm—until He takes me to my home in
heaven. Many waters cannot quench His love for me—
rivers cannot wash it away.*

KNOWN FOR HIS GREAT LOVE

usician Michael Card once said in an interview: "Again and again in China I talked to people who had never heard of Christianity, never heard of Jesus, never heard a single word from the Bible. Yet through nature and their God-given conscience, many believed in God. Not only did they believe God existed, they had derived some understanding about His loving character because He provided food, water, and a beautiful world. One old woman said, 'I've known Him for years. I just didn't know His name.'"[1]

God's tender mercies are available to all people—and that includes you—this day. He wants to meet whatever need you have. He is love and is known by His loving character. Trust Him to be faithful in your life!

The Lord is gracious and compassionate,
  slow to anger and rich in love.
The Lord is good to all;
  He has compassion on all he has made.

PSALM 145:8–9

DECLARATION FOR YOUR LIFE

My Father shows His unyielding compassion for me by clothing me in His unmerited and gainful favor.

He is resonant in His love towards me, showing His patience and understanding every day of my life.

He is not easily angered and is always there to help me when I need Him. He will not turn away from me no matter what I have done. The second I turn to Him, He embraces me and brings me out of the devil's hold.

He longs to do good things for me. He is not only good to me some of the time, but He is good to me all of the time.

A Prayer for God's Presence

ord,

Thank You for Your continual presence in my life. Help me to be continually sensitive to the surprising places where You want to meet me. I call upon You today in truth—I need to hear Your voice, to feel Your touch.

I place my trust in You, knowing that You hold my life safely in Your hands. Whatever happens in this life, I know You can help me to overcome. You will not give me more than what You and I can handle—together.

In Jesus' name I pray,

Amen.

The Lord is near to all who call upon Him,
To all who call upon Him in truth.
He will fulfill the desire of those who
fear Him;
He also will hear their cry and save them.
The Lord preserves all who love Him,
But all the wicked He will destroy.

PSALM 145:18–20 NKJV

DECLARATION FOR YOUR LIFE

My heart belongs to God and His to me. We bring great joy to each other in this life. He fulfills my every desire and is always there to take His stand at my side. His eyes never leave me, nor do mine leave Him. We two are dedicated to our covenant, and our love for each other will never run dry.

any people revere Francis of Assisi, the 13th-century saint known for his simple lifestyle and deep love for the poor. He founded the Franciscan order, restored numerous chapels, and helped countless needy people. What most people don't know, however, is that Francis spent most of his life not in doing good works, but in a love relationship with God, established in prayer.

The Father loves you so much that He longs to spend time with you in prayer. And as in the life of Francis of Assisi, the outgrowth of your prayer life with Him will benefit untold numbers of people. Have you told the Lord today that you love Him? He is waiting to tell the same to you.

Let the morning bring me word of your
    unfailing love,
  for I have put my trust in you.
Show me the way I should go,
  for to you I lift up my soul.

PSALM 143:8

DECLARATION FOR YOUR LIFE

*The very morning brings me word of my Father's
unfailing love for me. He never fails to be there for me.
He makes certain that I understand the direction I
must take.*

OF COURSE, GOD CAN FIX IT!

hile in the Philippines, Allen admired the artisans' exquisite workmanship and took home a souvenir—a pure silver money clip embellished with a distinctive design. Allen carried that clip for the next twenty-four years. One day it finally broke as he slipped a few bills into it.

Eventually Allen took the two pieces of the clip back to the silversmith in the Philippines. He explained his predicament and laid the pieces in the workman's outstretched hand. "I designed this clip. I was the only one to make these."

"Can you fix it?" Allen asked.

"I made it. Of course, I can fix it!" the silversmith said.

Whatever need you have today, God, your Creator, in His love is willing to "fix it." He can—and He will.

If you will diligently hearken to the voice of
the Lord your God and will do what is right
in His sight, and will listen to and obey His
commandments and keep all His statutes, I
will put none of the diseases upon you
which I brought upon the Egyptians,
for I am the Lord Who heals you.

Exodus 15:26 AMP

DECLARATION FOR YOUR LIFE

*I have a covenant with God. I diligently listen, giving
my complete attention to His Word, and I do what is
right in His sight. My ear is open to His voice, and I
am prepared to follow His commands. I have His word
that no disease can come upon me, which is brought
upon the world; for my God is Jehovah Rapha, the God
who heals me. He is the Lord of my health.*

aniel Webster, a nineteenth-century lawyer and statesman, was courting his wife-to-be, Grace Fletcher. As he held skeins of silk thread for her, he suggested, "Grace, we've been engaged in untying knots; let's see if we can tie a knot that would be almost impossible to untie." Grace accepted Webster's proposal.

After they had both passed away, their children found a little box marked "Precious Documents." Among the contents were letters of courtship and a tiny silk knot—one that had never been untied.

Because you know Jesus and He is the Lord of your life, nothing this world sends your way can ever separate you from His love. Just as the knot Daniel and his wife tied, God is tied to you, committed to loving you and helping you no matter what happens.

I am convinced that neither death nor life,
neither angels nor demons, neither the
present nor the future, nor any powers,
neither height nor depth, nor anything
else in all creation, will be able to
separate us from the love of God
that is in Christ Jesus our Lord.

ROMANS 8:38-39

DECLARATION FOR YOUR LIFE

It doesn't matter what my situation may be. It doesn't matter if I am facing death, or looked upon as a sheep headed for the slaughter. No matter what is going on in my life, I shall rise as more than a conqueror through Him who loves me!

THE RAGGEDY DOLL

n Christmas morning, little Amy was delighted to find a new doll under the tree. "She's so pretty!" she squealed in excitement as she hugged her new toy. Then rushing to hug her grandmother, the giver of the doll, she cried, "Thank you, thank you!"

Amy played with her new doll most of the day, but toward evening she sought out one of her old dolls. Its nose was broken, one eye was askew, and an arm was missing. "Well," Grandma noted, "it seems as if you like the old dolly better."

"I like the beautiful doll," Amy replied, "but I love this old doll more, because if I didn't love her, no one else would."

No matter how you feel about yourself, God loves you. He sees great and wonderful things in you. You are adored and cherished by Him!

Love is patient, love is kind. It does not envy, it does not boast, it is not proud.

1 Corinthians 13:4

Declaration for Your Life

My heavenly Father loves me with all of His heart. His very life is centered around His love for me. He is patient with me and kind towards me. He ever lives to do great things for me.

LOVE MADE YOU!

ichael Sellers once wrote: "The beasts of the sky say: 'Love made me.' The birds of the air say: 'Love made me.' The creatures that swim in the sea say: 'Love made me.' Only man, his back turned to the sun, does not say, 'Love made me.' But when he turns round in the love of Christ then he, too, knows in his heart 'Love made me' and he cries out with every living creature, 'Love made me! My Father in heaven loves me!'"[2]

Can you say the same thing? God loves you so much that He created you in His image, with the capacity to love and be loved by Him. Remind yourself of His amazing love often and be confident that He has good things in store for you. Love made you!

How great is the love the Father has
lavished on us, that we should be called
children of God! And that is what we are!

1 JOHN 3:1

DECLARATION FOR YOUR LIFE

*How great is the Father's love for me that I should be
called the son/daughter of God! And that is what I
am! I am now God's own son/daughter!*

E. Marsh once listed just a few of the many blessings God pours out on His children:

An acceptance that can never be questioned (Ephesians 1:6).

An inheritance that can never be lost (1 Peter 1:3–5).

A deliverance that can never be excelled (2 Corinthians 1:10).

A grace that can never be limited (2 Corinthians 12:9).

A hope that can never be disappointed (Hebrews 6:18–19).

A joy that can never be diminished (John 15:11).

A peace that can never be disturbed (John 14:27).

A righteousness that can never be tarnished (2 Corinthians 5:21).

A salvation that can never be canceled (Hebrews 5:9).[3]

All those blessings belong to you. Allow your faith to embrace these powerful truths today.

God, who is rich in mercy, for his
great love wherewith he loved us,
Even when we were dead in sins, hath
quickened us together with Christ.

EPHESIANS 2:4-5 KJV

DECLARATION FOR YOUR LIFE

*Because of the great love that He has for me, God, who
is rich in mercy, made me alive with Christ.*

he team captains are down to their last grudging choices: a slow kid for catcher and someone to stick out in right field where nobody hits the ball. They choose the last ones two at a time—"you and you"—because it makes no difference. And the remaining kids they deal for as handicaps: "If I take him, then you gotta take him," they say.

Did you ever think about the fact that you are so valuable to God that He "chose you early"—with enthusiasm? If God is for you, who could possibly be against you?

If ye were of the world, the world would love his own: but because ye are not of the world, but I have chosen you out of the world, therefore the world hateth you.

JOHN 15:19 KJV

DECLARATION FOR YOUR LIFE

I am not of this world. I have been chosen out of the world and am no longer subject to its ways of living and being. I have become one with Him in all things and I follow Him with my whole heart.

Made into Poetry

 esus the Son left heaven and came to this earth to prove to you that God the Father loves you just as you are! An ironsmith once said that he loved to work with iron as a metal because it was so hard to bend into something beautiful. His challenge was to "make iron into poetry."

We are like that with our sins. Before Jesus comes to dwell within us, we are rigid and do not bend easily. But when the Holy Spirit takes charge of our lives, we become molded into His image. God's love changes us into who He wants us to become—His beloved children, in whom His love dwells and upon whom His love is showered.

[Jesus prayed], "Righteous Father, though the
world does not know you, I know you,
and they know that you have sent me.
I have made you known to them, and will
continue to make you known in order that
the love you have for me may be in them
and that I myself may be in them."

JOHN 17:25–26

DECLARATION FOR YOUR LIFE

*Jesus has made the Father known to me, revealing to me
His very character and the reality of His love towards
me. The love that He gives to Jesus, He now gives to me
as well, and Jesus Himself dwells within me.*

GOD'S LOVE IS FOREVER

 n August 16, 1987, Northwest Airlines flight 225 crashed just after taking off from the Detroit airport, killing 155 people. One survived: a four-year-old from Tempe, Arizona, named Cecelia.

News accounts say that when rescuers found Cecelia, they thought she had been in one of the cars on the highway where the plane had crashed. But when the passenger register for the flight was checked, there she was.

Cecelia survived because, even as the plane was falling, her mother unbuckled her own seatbelt, got on her knees in front of her daughter, wrapped her arms and body around Cecelia, and wouldn't let go.

Nothing could separate that child from her parent's love—neither tragedy nor disaster, neither the fall nor the flames that followed, neither life nor death.

Such is the love of God for you! Jesus left heaven, came to the earth, and covered you with His sacrifice so that you can live with Him forever.

Who shall separate us from the love
of Christ?

ROMANS 8:35

DECLARATION FOR YOUR LIFE

*Who is it that can separate me from God's love?
Can persecution, troubles, hardship, famine, depres-
sion, distress, peril, or danger separate me from
Jesus' love? No!!!*

ot only does God love you as His own child, adopting you into His wonderful family, He has made amazing promises to you in His Word, promises that He is committed to fulfilling in your life. He has not only made these promises, but He stands *ready* to perform them, to cause them to come to pass in incredible, sometimes surprising ways. God, who cannot and does not lie, has promised you that His goodness will follow you, His child, all the days of your life. All He asks is that you trust in Him. God longs to bless you. If you're ready, He is too!

It shall come to pass, that before
they call, I will answer; and while
they are yet speaking, I will hear.

Isaiah 65:24 KJV

Declaration for Your Life

*When I call upon God, He answers me. He is so atten-
tive to my prayers that before I even speak, He has the
answer ready for me. I am God's son/daughter and
neither harm nor destruction can come near me. I have
His Word on it.*

A Prayer for Peace

 ear heavenly Father,

I thank You that You have poured out Your Spirit upon my life, and that one of the effects of Your love is peace. I claim righteousness, peace, and joy to fill my life as the fruit of my relationship with You.

As I wait on You, Lord, I pray that You will be my strength and defense and fulfill Your Word in every area of my life. I know that where the Spirit of the Lord is, there is peace.

Thank You for Your love and for the peace that passes all understanding.

In Jesus' name I pray. Amen.

Lord, you establish peace for us; all that we have accomplished you have done for us.

ISAIAH 26:12

DECLARATION FOR YOUR LIFE

My heavenly Father has ordained peace, favor, and an abundance of blessings for me. He has worked in and through me to achieve all that I have done. What a privilege it is to be in such an incredible partnership!

GOD'S HEALING POWER

 our Father, the eternal God, is your Healer, your Refuge, and your Habitation. He has sent His Word and healed you from every disease! His everlasting arms hold you as a loving Father holds his child.

The Lord has driven the enemy from before you, and He has charged you with destroying the strongholds of the enemy in this earth.

Give thanks and praise to Him today that you live in safety and health under your Father's protection and care and live in the land of abundance that He has promised to you and to your children!

He sent His word and healed them,

And delivered them from their destructions.

Oh, that men would give thanks to the Lord
for His goodness,

And for His wonderful works to the children
of men!

PSALM 107:20–21 NKJV

DECLARATION FOR YOUR LIFE

*God has sent His Word into this earth to heal me and
rescue me from death. His love for me never fails. He is
always working to bring good things into my life and
perform mighty deeds on my behalf.*

party of pioneers on the Oregon Trail suffered for weeks from a scarcity of water and grass for their animals. Most of the wagons had broken down, causing endless delays in the stifling heat.

One night the leaders called a meeting to air complaints. When they gathered around the campfire, one man stood up and said, "Before we commence our complaints, don't you think we should at least first thank God that He has brought us this far with no loss of life, and that we have strength to finish our journey?"

The other settlers agreed. After the brief prayer, all that could be heard was silence, because no one had any grievances they felt were important enough to voice.

Be thankful today for all of the blessings your loving Creator has poured upon your life.

Let them give thanks to the Lord for his
  unfailing love
 and his wonderful deeds for men,
for he satisfies the thirsty
 and fills the hungry with good things.

PSALM 107:8–9

DECLARATION FOR YOUR LIFE

I praise my Father for His goodness towards me. He is not good to me only some of the time; He is good to me all of the time! His wonderful works of kindness toward me have no end. He satisfies my longing soul! He fills my hungry soul with His favor and loving-kindness forevermore!

YOU ARE LOVED BY GOD!

ne evening, while putting her daughter, Kayley, to bed, Carla asked her what it was like to be four years old. "It's special," little Kayley replied.

"Why is it special?" Carla asked.

Kayley responded, "It's special because I know that my mommy loves me."

God the Father has called you into fellowship with Him and with His Son, Jesus Christ. As you participate in a close and intimate relationship with Him, you will walk in the light of His presence and live in the knowledge of His great love for you.

What a profound thought! If we would just take the time, we would see, like Kayley, that life is special because our heavenly Father loves us so very much!

The Lord God is a Sun and Shield;
the Lord bestows [present] grace and favor
and [future] glory (honor, splendor, and
heavenly bliss)! No good thing will He
withhold from those who walk uprightly.

Psalm 84:11 amp

Declaration for Your Life

My Father is my sun and shield. He enlightens and enlivens me as I do His will, and He protects me from danger so that I remain secure. He bestows on me His favor and honor, and I am held in high esteem by my peers. No good thing will He withhold from me as I daily walk in His ways.

ohn had, in childhood, been an altar boy, his family very active in the church. Unfortunately, John got involved in the drug culture and ended up homeless, on the streets. Eventually, he called his former pastor for assistance.

The pastor rescued the young man, took him home, and fed him. As he ate, the pastor asked if John had ever asked Christ for help in his troubles, to which John replied, brightening, "You know, when I get myself back together, that's when I'll ask Jesus for help."

God doesn't want you to wait until you "get your act together" before you come to Him. He longs to take you, just as you are, and transform your life and circumstances to shine forth His glory!

For You, Lord, are good, and ready to forgive,
And abundant in mercy to all those who call
upon You.

PSALM 86:5 NKJV

DECLARATION FOR YOUR LIFE

God forgives me of all of my shortcomings. His love for me is boundless. I can expect nothing but good things from Him.

few years ago, a family attended a Star Trek convention, marveling at all the fans dressed up as characters from the television series. One fan, who was costumed as a half-black-half-white alien, caught four-year-old Rebecca's eye. Thinking of her favorite children's chorus, "Jesus Loves the Little Children," she remarked, "Jesus thinks that one is precious." Then she added hopefully, "Do you think we'll see any red and yellows?"

No matter who you are or the color of your skin, God adores you. Just as He created all the people of the world, He created you for a specific purpose, which He is committed to carrying out in your life!

Blessed are those you choose
and bring near to live in your courts!
We are filled with the good things of
    your house,
  of your holy temple.
You answer us with awesome deeds
    of righteousness,
  O God our Savior,
the hope of all the ends of the earth
  and of the farthest seas.

PSALM 65:4–5

DECLARATION FOR YOUR LIFE

My Father has chosen me and adopted me as His own child. He has brought me near to Himself and has given me a place of honor in the courts of His palace. He fills me with all good things so that I am in need of nothing. All I have to do is ask and He freely gives me all that He has.

ust as a husband and a wife live out their lives against the backdrop of being married, so we live out the entirety of our lives against the backdrop of a constant relationship with God. He is always there, always loving us, always ready to listen to us. As we recognize His unwavering commitment to us, we are able to live in the day-to-day adventure and challenge of His presence. It's as if we constantly say, "Oh, I can't wait to talk to Him about this!"

Whatever your concerns or anxieties are today, the Lord stands ready to listen—and to respond. As His very own dearly loved child, place yourself in the position to receive His blessings. It's the fruit of your relationship with Him!

Cast your burden on the Lord,
And He shall sustain you;
He shall never permit the righteous to
   be moved.

DECLARATION FOR YOUR LIFE

*I cast all of my cares and anxieties upon the Lord and
He faithfully supports me. He will never allow me to be
overcome by my enemies or be shaken to the point of
despair. In Him, I rest secure for all of eternity.*

ecause God is near, there is nothing to fear. He is the All-Sufficient One, the great Need-Meeter, and in His presence, nothing can harm us or trouble us in any way.

God has been this comfort to all those who have believed in Him, who put their faith in Him despite their circumstances. These words of Julian of Norwich, penned in medieval times, echo our own confession today:

God, of Your goodness, give me Yourself; for You are sufficient for me. I cannot properly ask anything less, to be worthy of You. In You alone, I have everything I need. In You is everything I know to be good. In Your love, You clothe me, enfold, and embrace me; that tender love completely surrounds me, never to leave me. Amen.

Do not fear, for I am with you;
  do not be dismayed, for I am your God.
I will strengthen you and help you;
  I will uphold you with my righteous
    right hand.

\textsc{Isaiah 41:10}

Declaration for Your Life

I have no cause for fear, for my God is with me. I will not be dismayed, for God is my Father and He has promised to never leave me, nor forsake me. He strengthens me and assists me in every circumstance. He upholds me with His righteous right hand so that my victory is made certain.

GOD GIVES GOOD GIFTS!

ill Hybels once said:

"You don't have to pester God to get His attention. You don't have to grovel. If one of my kids called me and said, 'Daddy, please, please, I beg of you, I'm pleading with you to listen to my need,' I'd say, 'Time out! I don't like the assumption here. You don't have to go through all these gymnastics. What can I do for you? Nothing in my life is more important than you!'

"What could possibly give me greater pleasure in life than meeting the needs of my children? What?"[4]

What could give God greater pleasure than meeting the needs of you, His child?

[Jesus said], "Which of you, if his son asks for bread, will give him a stone? Or if he asks for a fish, will give him a snake? If you, then, though you are evil, know how to give good gifts to your children, how much more will your Father in heaven give good gifts to those who ask him!"

MATTHEW 7:9–11

DECLARATION FOR YOUR LIFE

My heavenly Father loves me and is always good to me. If I ask Him for a loaf of bread, He does not offer me a stone instead. If I ask Him for a fish, He does not give me a snake. To the contrary, He is more than willing to give me specifically what I persistently ask for. When He sees that my heart is set on it, He makes sure that I have it.

hen we come to God and say, "I love You, and I'm prepared to do Your will, whatever You want me to do," we can be sure that God is not going to make us miserable! Rather, He rejoices and fits our lives into His pattern for us, into that place where He, in His great omniscience and love, knows that we will fit—hand in glove.

If we ask for bread, will He give us a stone? Certainly not! He, our Father, our Creator, who made us and who knows us better than we know ourselves, is the One to whom we pray. He is filled with love for His children and has only blessings to bestow!

We are bound to give thanks always to God
for you, brethren beloved of the Lord,
because God hath from the beginning chosen
you to salvation through sanctification of the
Spirit and belief of the truth: Whereunto he
called you by our gospel, to the obtaining
of the glory of our Lord Jesus Christ.

2 THESSALONIANS 2:13–14 KJV

DECLARATION FOR YOUR LIFE

*I am deeply loved by the Lord. From the beginning, He
chose me to be saved through the sanctifying work of
the Holy Spirit and through my belief in the Truth. He
called me to this through the Gospel, so that I might
share in the glory of my Lord Jesus Christ.*

hen Juanita was staying with a neighbor's five- and seven-year-olds, she heard a squeal coming from the next room, and then Becky's voice. "Mike, God doesn't love you when you do things like that!"

Mike's voice rang out, "Yes, He does, too, love me! He's ... He's just disappointed in me!"

No matter what you may have done in your life, there is nothing that can stand in the way of God's love for you. God's grace is not only sufficient to cover your sins, it's versatile too. He accepts and loves each one of us just as we are—and He gives us the immense privilege of demonstrating our gratitude to Him by loving each other the same way! Allow Him to teach you to receive His love and then pass it along to the people He places in your path.

May the Master take you by the
hand and lead you along the path of
God's love and Christ's endurance.

2 Thessalonians 3:5 The Message

Declaration for Your Life

The Lord continually directs my heart into the Father's love, showing me how to trust and walk in it, and into the steadfast patience of Christ, which is a sure confidence in my inevitable victory.

A PERSONAL MESSAGE

t the seven o'clock Christmas Eve service, a little girl came out and pulled on her pastor's robe. "What can I do for you, Emily?" he asked.

"This is for you, Pastor Harrington," she replied, handing him a small scrap of paper.

When he opened it, he saw that it read, "I love you."

Like that note, God sent His Son, Jesus, into this earth to give us the message of His amazing, divine love. And the message has been personalized: "It's for you." Through Jesus, grace and peace have not only been added unto you—but they have been multiplied! Not only that, His love, grace, and peace are for each one of us *individually*. How incredible!

Grace and peace be yours in abundance through the knowledge of God and of Jesus our Lord. His divine power has given us everything we need for life and godliness.

2 PETER 1:2–3

DECLARATION FOR YOUR LIFE

Grace and peace are mine in abundance through the knowledge of God and of Jesus Christ my Lord. Through His divine power I have been given all things that pertain unto life and godliness. These things He has bestowed upon me through my deep and personal knowledge of Him who has called me into His own glory and goodness.

ne young resident student had a marvelous effect on the children in his care at a local hospital. They responded to him with delight. The staff assigned a nurse to discover what the secret of this young resident was. It wasn't until the second week when she was on night duty that she learned what was going on. Every night on his last round, the student would kiss, hug, and tuck in every one of the children. It was in that act of compassion and sympathy that he reached out to the kids—just as the compassion and sympathy of Jesus has reached out to us in ways we could never have dreamed of.

Napoleon Bonaparte once said: "Alexander, Caesar, and Hannibel may have conquered the world, but they had no friends. Jesus founded His empire upon love, and at this hour, millions would die for Him. He has won the hearts of men, a task a conqueror cannot do."

Has the love of God won *your* heart today?

This is how we know what love is: Jesus
Christ laid down his life for us. And we
ought to lay down our lives for our brothers.

1 John 3:16

Declaration for Your Life

*This is how I know what love is: Jesus Christ laid
down His life for me. In light of this, I will lay down
my life for the Church.*

he story is told of a town where all the residents are ducks. Every Sunday the ducks waddle out of their houses and waddle down Main Street to their church. The duck minister comes forward and opens the duck Bible: "Ducks! God has given you wings! With wings you can fly! With wings you can mount up and soar like eagles!" All the ducks shout, "Amen!" *And then they all waddle back home.*

God's will is that you would receive *all* of the blessings that He has prepared for you. His great love has made provision for you to walk in these blessings, so don't waddle—learn how to fly above your circumstances and live the victorious life He has called you to live!

Blessed be the God and Father of our
Lord Jesus Christ, who has blessed us
with every spiritual blessing in the
heavenly places in Christ.

EPHESIANS 1:3 NKJV

DECLARATION FOR YOUR LIFE

*I give all praise, honor, and glory to my God, the
Father of my Lord Jesus Christ, for He has blessed me
with every spiritual blessing in Christ. I choose to
stand on His Word and actively claim these blessings
to be mine in Jesus' name.*

hortly after Mike and his wife became Christians, the IRS asked him to defend a tax return from years earlier. Unfortunately, he hadn't been honest, and so began months of painful meetings with the IRS.

The day of the last meeting, after parking, Mike discovered the meter wouldn't take his coins. He was already late, and he prayed, *Lord, I'm trusting You for a huge tax problem. It's dumb not to trust You with this little meter.*

When he came out later, he saw a piece of paper on his car. Stunned, he prayed, *Lord, I asked for Your help!* But when he came closer, he saw a note from a friend: "Mike, your time was expired. I took care of it."

God cares about every detail of your life—from the big things to the smallest. Trust His loving-kindness to care for you throughout the day in every situation that you face.

What is man that you are mindful of him,
the son of man that you care for him?
You made him a little lower than the
heavenly beings
and crowned him with glory and honor.
You made him ruler over the works of
your hands;
you put everything under his feet.

PSALM 8:4–6

DECLARATION FOR YOUR LIFE

God is ever mindful of me and cares for me with unwavering diligence. He has created me to be just short of divine (Elohim; God; heavenly beings) and has crowned me with glory and honor.

od's protection is made known as we remember those times when we have experienced His faithfulness in our lives. Every answered prayer, every victory, every storm that has been calmed in His presence helps us to keep from falling or losing hope when we do face trials or difficulties.

As you grow in the kingdom of God and in the experience of His love, realize that each victory, each triumph of your faith, brings a new awareness of how much He cares for you. It is a stepping-stone toward your ultimate goal of finishing the race and receiving the crown of glory that He is waiting to give to you!

I call on you, O God, for you will answer me;
    give ear to me and hear my prayer.
Show the wonder of your great love,
    you who save by your right hand
    those who take refuge in you. …
Keep me as the apple of your eye;
    hide me in the shadow of your wings.

PSALM 17:6–8

DECLARATION FOR YOUR LIFE

I am held secure in the arms of my Father. When I call to Him, He hears me and rescues me from all oppression. He keeps me as the apple of His eye and hides me in the shadow of His wings. The Lord cherishes me and holds me dear to His heart. He stills my hunger and supplies me with an abundance of provisions.

ne fall afternoon, an elderly man was at home with his wife and heard a knock at the door. The visitor was a neighbor who said to the man, "I was out feeding my horses and I felt like God was prompting me to come and say thank you for the difference you've made in my life."

She sat down and began to tell stories about times when the man had been merciful to her, and she thanked him for his help throughout the years. The man paused, looked at her, and said, "It was the Lord Jesus Christ who did it."

When you help other people and engage in small acts of kindness, you allow the Lord to work through your hands and your feet. And when someone performs an act of kindness for you, learn to recognize it as the grace of God overflowing into your life. It is the Lord Jesus Christ who does it!

Give thanks to the Lord, for he is good;
   his love endures forever.

PSALM 107:1

DECLARATION FOR YOUR LIFE

My Father is good to me. His mercy and loving-kindness toward me endure forever!

he greatest spiritual task facing us is to so fully trust that we belong to God that we can be free in the world—free to speak even when our words are not received kindly; free to act even when our words are criticized or considered useless; free to receive love from others and from God and to be grateful for all of the signs of God's presence in the world. We are truly able to love the world when we fully believe that we are loved far beyond its boundaries.

"Only he who can say, 'The Lord is the strength of my life,' can say, 'Of whom shall I be afraid?'"[5]

The Lord is my light and my salvation;
whom shall I fear? the Lord is the strength of
my life; of whom shall I be afraid?

PSALM 27:1 KJV

DECLARATION FOR YOUR LIFE

*The Lord is my light and my salvation—I shall fear
no one. The very Creator of the universe is the impene-
trable fortress of safety in my life.*

A Prayer for Shelter and Help

ear heavenly Father,

I thank You that You are my hiding place, and that I can run to You in troubled times and You will shelter me.

Lord, the world can be such a confusing and dangerous place, and at times it is difficult to know the right path to take. I thank You for Your calm, reassuring voice in times of distress. I thank You for the Holy Spirit who will guide me into all truth. I thank You that You preserve my life from trouble and surround me with songs of deliverance from anyone or anything that would cause me harm.

I will trust You to counsel me and watch over my life. I know that You will perform Your Word over me, and that Your unfailing love will surround me all of my days.

In Jesus' name I pray. Amen.

You are my hiding place;
You shall preserve me from trouble;
You shall surround me with songs
    of deliverance.

PSALM 32:7 NKJV

DECLARATION FOR YOUR LIFE

God is my very hiding place against all harmful attacks. He shelters me in a hedge of protection. He preserves me from trouble and surrounds me with songs of deliverance. It is the God of all the universe, my own heavenly Father, who counsels and watches over me with a relentless eye. His unfailing love ever surrounds me.

he *Chronicles of Narnia* are wonderful children's stories about the land of Narnia. In the second book, *Prince Caspian*, Lucy enters Narnia again, and she hasn't seen Aslan, the lion figure representing Christ, in quite some time. The two have a wonderful reunion, in which Lucy says to the lion, "Aslan, You're bigger now!"

Aslan replies, "Lucy, that's because you are older. You see, Lucy, every year that you grow, you will find Me bigger." Isn't that the case in our relationship with Christ? Every year we grow, we find Him bigger in His love, His grace, His goodness, His faithfulness, and in those promises that He has given to us. As Dwight L. Moody once said, "God has never made a promise that was too good to be true!"

O clap your hands, all ye people;
shout unto God with the voice of triumph.
For the Lord most high is terrible;
he is a great King over all the earth.

PSALM 47:1–2 KJV

DECLARATION FOR YOUR LIFE

I will praise my Father with my whole heart and all that is within me. I will clap my hands and shout to Him with a voice of triumph! He is the great King over all the earth.

HEAVENLY COMFORT

homas á Kempis once said, "A man ought to rest wholly upon God, so that he needeth not seek much comfort at the hands of men." While it is good for us to be comforted by other people, it is the Holy Spirit alone, the Great Comforter, who can heal the deepest hurts in our souls. Your Father longs to heal your broken heart. Trust in God completely to heal you—spirit, soul, and body. Run into His outstretched arms of love and experience the healing balm of His presence.

The Lord is near to those who have a
    broken heart,
And saves such as have a contrite spirit.
Many are the afflictions of the righteous,
But the Lord delivers him out of them all.

PSALM 34:18–19 NKJV

DECLARATION FOR YOUR LIFE

*My Father comforts me when I am brokenhearted.
When my spirit is crushed and I feel alone, He wraps
His tender arms around me and embraces me in His
love. I am faced with troubles of many kinds, but the
Lord delivers me out of every one.*

ou are safe when you rest in the presence of the Lord.

Corrie ten Boom, the famous survivor of the Nazi Holocaust, trusted in God and He brought her safely through some of the most horrific circumstances a person could possibly face. She said:

> *"When Jesus takes your hand, He holds you tight. When Jesus holds you tight, He leads you through your whole life. And when Jesus leads you through your whole life, He brings you safely home."*[6]

Allow Jesus to take your hand, and He will bring you safely through whatever you face this day.

The Lord redeems the soul of His servants,
And none of those who trust in Him shall
be condemned.

PSALM 34:22 NKJV

DECLARATION FOR YOUR LIFE

Through everything the world sends my way, I stand unscathed. I am a redeemed and reborn son/daughter of the living God! There is absolutely no condemnation for me, for I have taken my refuge in the Lord.

A Miraculous Healing

 page from the journal of John Wesley, the great evangelist and founder of the Methodist church:

"1741, May 10. Sunday, pain in back and head, with fever; had to lie down most of day; only easy in one position. At night, tried to preach; pain and seized with cough. There came to mind strongly, 'These signs shall follow them that believe.' Prayed; called on Jesus aloud to increase my faith and to confirm the Word of His grace. While I was speaking, my pain vanished away, the fever left me, my bodily strength returned, and for many weeks, I felt neither sickness nor pain. Unto Thee, O Lord, do I give thanks!"

Thank God today for His loving, healing touch!

Heal me, O Lord, and I shall be healed;
save me, and I shall be saved,
for You are my praise.

JEREMIAH 17:14 AMP

DECLARATION FOR YOUR LIFE

My trust and focus is on the Lord alone.

He has declared me to be healed; therefore, I am healed.

He has declared my salvation; therefore, I am saved.

ne day C. H. Spurgeon was walking through the English countryside with a friend. As they strolled along, the evangelist noticed a barn with a weather vane on its roof. At the top of the vane were these words: "GOD IS LOVE." Spurgeon remarked to his companion that he thought this was a rather inappropriate place for such a message. "Weather vanes are changeable," he said, "but God's love is constant."

"I don't agree with you about those words," his friend replied. "You misunderstood the meaning. That sign is indicating a truth: Regardless of which way the wind blows, God is love."

Everything that God does for you, He does out of love!

Behold, what manner of love the Father
hath bestowed upon us, that we
should be called the [children] of God.

1 John 3:1 kjv

Declaration for Your Life

*How great is the Father's love for me that I should
be called the son/daughter of God! And that is what
I am!*

W. Tozer once said, "With the goodness of God to desire our highest welfare, the wisdom of God to plan it, and the power of God to achieve it, what do we lack?" How profound!

As you trust in God with all your heart, He will provide for your every need. As a believer, you will lack nothing when you place yourself squarely in His hands. He redeems you from the power of darkness and brings you into His kingdom of light.

What do you lack today? Allow El Shaddai, the All-Sufficient One, to meet every need that you have.

My God shall supply all your need according
to his riches in glory by Christ Jesus.

PHILIPPIANS 4:19 KJV

DECLARATION FOR YOUR LIFE

*I have God's word that He will supply all of my
needs according to His riches in glory through Christ
Jesus. In this, I give glory to God, my Father, forevermore! Amen!*

sailor serving in the South Pacific during World War II was frightened and homesick. His way of life and all that had been familiar to him was gone, and he found himself living a strange life among strangers, unsure of his fate from moment to moment. Standing on the deck of his ship one night, he spotted the Big and Little Dippers—the same constellations he had studied in the blackened night skies back home in Ohio. Suddenly he felt at home and at peace, realizing the same sky as always was above him—and the same God as always was beside him.

God does not change. In all times and circumstances of your life, His promises remain faithful and true.

We should be saved from our enemies
And from the hand of all who hate us,
To perform the mercy promised to
   our fathers
And to remember His holy covenant,
The oath which He swore to our
   father Abraham.

LUKE 1:71–73 NKJV

DECLARATION FOR YOUR LIFE

*My Father establishes His covenant with me so that He
can show me His mercy, compassion, and loving-
kindness at all times and in every circumstance. All
that He has commanded and provided in His
covenant, He carries out on my behalf!*

omeone asked Dwight Moody how he managed to remain so intimate in his relationship with Christ. He replied, "I have come to Him as the best friend I have ever found, and I can trust Him in that relationship. I have believed He is Savior; I have believed He is God; I have believed He is my friend, and there isn't any problem in my life, there isn't any uncertainty in my work but I turn and speak to Him as naturally as to someone in the same room, and I have done it these years because I can trust Jesus."[7]

I am not ashamed, for I know whom
I have believed and am persuaded that
He is able to keep what I have committed
to Him until that Day.

2 TIMOTHY 1:12 NKJV

DECLARATION FOR YOUR LIFE

*I know the One in whom I have believed, and I am
convinced that He is able to guard what I have entrusted
to Him. He is trustworthy—I can count on Him!*

ccording to Charles Spurgeon, "The Christian knows no change with regard to God. He may be in happiness today, tomorrow he may be distressed; but there is never any change in his relationship with God. God is unchangeable! If He loved me yesterday, He loves me today. I am neither better nor worse in God than I ever was. I will never lose anything of what I have in Him."[8]

The One who guards your life never changes. His love for you is eternal!

My help comes from the Lord,
  the Maker of heaven and earth.
He will not let your foot slip—
  he who watches over you will
    not slumber;
indeed, he who watches over Israel
  will neither slumber nor sleep.

Psalm 121:2–4

Declaration for Your Life

My help comes from the Creator of heaven and earth! My destiny is fixed and I am resolved to attain it. My Father never sleeps or even blinks an eye. He is the shade at my right hand so that nothing can ever come close to harming me. He watches over my coming and my going, and everything in between, both now and forevermore!

E lisabeth Kubler-Ross, the famous grief counselor, once said about comfort, "I've never met a person whose greatest need was anything other than real, unconditional love. There is no mistaking love. You feel it in your heart. It is the common fiber of life, the flame that heats our soul, energizes our spirit, and supplies passion to our lives. It is our connection to God and to each other."

As you live out your life here on earth, know that you, God's amazing creation, are adored by God. You are loved unconditionally and comforted by Him, and you will find your greatest fulfillment by unconditionally loving and comforting others in return.

Praise be to the God and Father of our Lord
Jesus Christ, the Father of compassion and
the God of all comfort, who comforts us
in all our troubles, so that we can comfort
those in any trouble with the comfort
we ourselves have received from God.

2 Corinthians 1:3–4

Declaration for Your Life

My heavenly Father is the Father of mercies and the God of all comfort. His compassion towards me is boundless. He comforts, encourages, and assists me through all of life's troubles, so that I can comfort, encourage, and assist others who are going through the same things that I have gone through.

NOTES

1. Interview with Michael Card, *Discipleship Journal*, Nov./Dec. 2002, 72.

2. Michael Sellers, "The Word of God and the Wisdom of Man," *Christianity Today*, 30, no. 17.

3. Leslie B. Flynn, *19 Gifts of the Spirit*, (Wheaton, Ill.: Victor, 1975).

4. Bill Hybels, "God's Attitude Toward Prayer," *Preaching Today*, no. 97.

5. Alexander McClaren, *Christian Reader*, 32, no. 3.

6. Corrie ten Boom, *In My Father's House* (Old Tappan, NJ: Revell, 1976), 147.

7. William M. Anderson, *The Faith That Satisfies* (New York: Loizeaux Brothers, 1948), 165.

8. Charles Haddon Spurgeon, *Spurgeon's Sermons*, Vol. 2 (Grand Rapids, Mich.: Baker, 1983), 6.

God loves you—no matter who you are, no matter what your past. God loves you so much that He gave His one and only begotten Son for you. The Bible tells us that "...whoever believes in him shall not perish but have eternal life" (John 3:16). Jesus laid down His life and rose again so that we could spend eternity with Him in heaven and experience His absolute best on earth. If you would like to receive Jesus into your life, say the following prayer out loud and mean it from your heart.

Heavenly Father, I come to You admitting that I am a sinner. Right now, I choose to turn away from sin, and I ask You to cleanse me of all unrighteousness. I believe that Your Son, Jesus, died on the cross to take away my sins. I also believe that He rose again from the dead so that I might be forgiven of my sins and made righteous through faith in Him. I call upon the name of the Lord Jesus Christ to be the Savior and Lord of my life. Jesus, I choose to follow You and ask that You fill me with the power of the Holy Spirit. I declare that right now I am a child of God. I am free from sin and full of the righteousness of God. I am saved in Jesus' name.

If you prayed this prayer to receive Jesus Christ as your Savior for the first time, please contact us on the Web at **www.harrisonhouse.com** to receive a free book.

Or you may write to us at

Harrison House
P.O. Box 35035
Tulsa, Oklahoma 74153

Delight yourself in the Lord and he will give you the desires of your heart. (Psalm 37:4.)

Experience freedom and joy as you come to understand and accept that God is good and is ready to abundantly meet all your needs.

It is a simple truth that your heavenly Father cares for you, His child. But it is easy to allow doubts and anxieties to creep into your life when you focus on its challenges—extra expenses, setbacks, unexpected disappointments. However, as you keep your eyes focused on the One who promises to meet your every need and yes, fulfill even your desires—your hope returns and your faith soars!

Discover the peace that comes from trusting the promises of God and celebrating His goodness and generosity in your life.

Blessed by God • 1-57794-804-1

Available at bookstores everywhere
or visit **www.harrisonhouse.com**.

Celebrate God's grace in your life beginning today.

In a world that is oftentimes unkind and unloving, the good news is that a loving God has chosen you to be His own.

God knows you far better than you know yourself and has designed a specific destiny for you—something only you personally can fulfill. Even if you feel that you have missed your opportunity, know that God is not moved by time as we are. His purpose for your life is waiting. Embrace the love that God has for you. Be assured that when God calls you by name, He is also patient and persistent and is always ready when you are.

Chosen by God will help your spirit soar through daily reminders of just how much you matter to God.

Chosen by God • 1-57794-803-3
Available at bookstores everywhere
or visit **www.harrisonhouse.com**.

www.harrisonhouse.com

Fast. Easy. Convenient!

- ◆ New Book Information
- ◆ Look Inside the Book
- ◆ Press Releases
- ◆ Bestsellers
- ◆ Free E-News
- ◆ Author Biographies

- ◆ Upcoming Books
- ◆ Share Your Testimony
- ◆ Online Product Availability
- ◆ Product Specials
- ◆ Order Online

For the latest in book news and author information, please visit us on the Web at www.harrisonhouse.com. Get up-to-date pictures and details on all our powerful and life-changing products. Sign up for our e-mail newsletter, *Friends of the House*, and receive free monthly information on our authors and products including testimonials, author announcements, and more!

Harrison House—
Books That Bring Hope, Books That Bring Change

THE HARRISON HOUSE VISION

Proclaiming the truth and the power
Of the Gospel of Jesus Christ
With excellence;

Challenging Christians to
Live victoriously
Grow spiritually,
Know God intimately.